Deel

509.2
MOR
Morgan, N.
Famous scientists

JAN 2 4 1994

FAMOUS SCIENTISTS

Nina Morgan

Wayland

Famous people

Famous Artists
Famous Campaigners for Change
Famous Explorers
Famous Inventors
Famous Musicians
Famous Scientists

Picture acknowledgements
The publishers would like to thank the following for supplying pictures: Camera Press 38 (top), 43, 45; Bruce Coleman 14/Frans Lanting; Mary Evans 12, 16, 23, 27; Michael Holford 10, 11; Hutchison Picture Library 29/Christina Dudwea, 30/Nigel Sitwell; Mansell Collection 5, 8, 9, 21, 22; Science Photo Library 6/J-L Charmet, 7, 13/Dr Jeremy Burgess, 17/J-L Charmet, l8/National Library of Medicine, 19/National Library of Medicine, 20/J-L Charmet, 26/Julian Baum, 31/Thomas Hollyman, 32/Astrid and Hanns-Frieder Michler, 37/Peter Menzel, 38/Chemical Design Ltd, 39/Science Source, 40/CERN, 41/Los Alamos National Library, 42/NASA, 44 (top)/Julian Baum, 44 (bottom)/Dr Rob Stepney; Topham Picture Library cover, 28, 33, 34, 35, 36; Wayland Picture Library cover, 4, 15, 24, 25. Cover artwork by Peter Dennis.

Series editor: Rosemary Ashley
Book editor: Paul Bennett
Series designer: Malcolm Walker

First published in 1993 by
Wayland (Publishers) Limited
6l Western Road, Hove
East Sussex, BN3 lJD, England

British Library Cataloguing in Publication Data
Morgan, Nina
   Famous Scientists. -(Famous People Series)
   I. Title   II. Series
   509.22

ISBN 0-7502-0669-1

Typeset by Kudos Editorial and Design Services
Printed and bound in Italy by Rotolito Lombardo S.p.A, Milan

Contents

Introduction

When talking about science, Albert Einstein once said that 'imagination is more important than knowledge'. Although they worked in different areas of science and at different times, the twelve scientists discussed in this book all shared a common bond of imagination, and the kind of curiosity that led them to explore the ideas they dreamed about.

Isaac *Newton*

The first modern scientist

Isaac Newton dedicated himself to science throughout his life and became one of the greatest scientists of all time. He thought deeply about how natural events, or phenomena, might be explained. His most famous book, *Principia*, is probably the greatest single work of science ever written, and contains his work on the laws of motion and the theory of gravitation. His theory of gravitation helped to explain the motion of the planets and the orbits of comets.

After an uncle persuaded Isaac Newton's mother that he had an 'extraordinary talent', Newton was sent to study mathematics at Cambridge University in 1660. Having obtained his degree, Newton returned to his mother's home in Lincolnshire to avoid an outbreak of the Great Plague.

Isaac Newton became one of the greatest scientists of all time. His theories are still used by physicists today.

By passing a beam of sunlight through a prism, Newton was able to show that white light is made up of all the colours of the rainbow.

During the eighteen months he spent in Lincolnshire, Newton made some of the greatest discoveries in the history of science. He invented a new mathematical technique which is now called calculus. He also began experimenting with light and lenses and discovered the nature of white light by passing a beam of sunlight through a prism. When Newton returned to Cambridge in 1667, his work so impressed the authorities that he was named professor of mathematics, although he was only twenty-six years old.

Towards the end of his life, Newton told his friends that the idea for his theory of gravitation first came to him as he sat in the garden of his family home, and saw an apple fall off a tree.

Newton also used his time in Lincolnshire to reflect on the forces that control the movement of objects. It is said that Newton first began to think about this question when he saw an apple drop from a tree. He decided that this must be because the earth attracted the apple, and this led him to work out the theory of gravitation. This started him thinking about the planets and how they move around the sun. Newton thought about this problem for many years.

In 1687, Newton published his book, *Principia*, in which he showed how a single set of laws could be used to explain the movement of the sun and the planets and the motion of objects on Earth. Newton's laws of motion still form the basis of much of science. *Principia* also contained Newton's ideas about gravity and the workings of the universe. He thought that gravity was the single force that holds the universe together, and all the bodies in it together.

Newton's work is important not only for what he discovered, but also for the methods he used to make his discoveries. He was one of the first people to use what we now consider to be 'scientific' methods. He based his theories on careful observation, and then tested and cross-checked them until he was certain that they were correct. 'Good' science is still carried out using these methods today.

Dates

1642 born at Woolsthorpe, Lincolnshire, England
1661 begins studies at Cambridge University
1665 returns to Lincolnshire to escape the plague; develops ideas about calculus, optics and gravity
1667 returns to Cambridge
1669 becomes Lucasian Professor of Mathematics at Cambridge
1687 *Principia* published
1727 dies

PHILOSOPHIÆ

NATURALIS

PRINCIPIA

MATHEMATICA.

Autore *J S. NEWTON*, *Trin. Coll. Cantab. Soc.* Matheseos Professore *Lucasiano*, & Societatis Regalis Sodali.

IMPRIMATUR·
S. P E P Y S, *Reg. Soc.* P R Æ S E S.
Julii 5. 1686.

L O N D I N I,

Juſſu *Societatis Regiæ* ac Typis *Joſephi Streater*. Proſtat apud plures Bibliopolas. *Anno* MDCLXXXVII.

Newton's book, Principia, was published in 1687. In it he explained his work on the laws of motion, the theory of tides and the theory of gravitation.

7

Michael *Faraday*

The father of modern electricity

Although Michael Faraday's work in chemistry was important – he discovered the chemical benzene and made a special study of the gas chlorine – it was his work on electricity and magnetism that made him famous. His discovery that a moving magnetic field can produce an electric current opened the way for the production of electrical power on a large scale. Today's huge machines, or generators, for making electricity for our homes, offices and factories, use the principles that Faraday discovered.

Michael Faraday was born at Newington, now in south London, the son of a blacksmith. At the age of fourteen, he was apprenticed as a bookbinder and his interest in science developed when he began reading the scientific books and magazines which customers brought in to be bound. In 1812, he began attending science lectures at the Royal Institution in London.

Michael Faraday's work on electricity and magnetism led directly to the generation of electricity and the electric motor.

At the lectures, Faraday met the famous scientist Sir Humphrey Davy and was offered a job as his laboratory assistant at the Royal Institution. While he was working with Davy, Faraday began to carry out experiments in chemistry. In 1823, he became the first person to produce liquid chlorine gas, and the following year he discovered the chemical benzene. He also invented a type of heat-proof glass.

After hearing of the work of the Danish scientist Hans Christian Oersted, who showed, in 1820, that an electric current could be used to produce a magnetic field, Faraday turned his attention to electricity. He soon had the idea that a magnetic field might be used to produce an electric current and set to work to see if that was possible.

As a young man, Faraday developed his interest in science by listening to lectures at the Royal Institution in London. After making many discoveries about both chemistry and electricity, Faraday was invited to give lectures at the Royal Institution.

First of all, Faraday worked to find a way to make electricity and magnetism work together to produce movement and, by 1830, he had developed the first electric motor. Then in 1831, after carrying out hundreds of experiments, he found that he could produce an electric current by moving a wire between the poles of a magnet. The electricity generated by this method is called alternating current – the current moves first in one direction, and then in the other. The electricity produced by batteries is different. It is called direct current and it flows in only one direction. Faraday's discovery opened the way for the production of electric current on a much larger scale and

Right   Faraday spent his scientific career studying chemistry and carrying out experiments on electricity and magnetism in this laboratory at the Royal Institution in London.

In the course of his work on electricity and magnetism, Faraday experimented with this disk dynamo to produce an electric current.

provided the basis for the huge generators which produce the electricity that we have in our homes and factories today.

Faraday went on to develop the transformer, a device that changes electrical energy from one voltage to another, and to prove that all electricity is the same, no matter what its source. He also investigated the effect of electricity on chemicals, and the effect that magnetism has on rays of some kinds of light. His discoveries were based on careful observation and experiments, a method used by scientists today.

Faraday won many honours and prizes for his work. When he died in 1867 at the age of seventy-six, he left behind a wealth of discoveries in chemistry and electricity which have changed our lives.

Dates

1791 born in London, England
1805 apprenticed as a bookbinder
1813 appointed as an assistant to Sir Humphry Davy at the Royal Institution, London
1830 discovers the principle of the electric motor
1831 discovers the principle of the transformer and the dynamo
1832 proves electricity is the same, no matter what its source
1867 dies

Charles *Darwin*

Evolution and the origin of species

Charles Darwin put forward the idea that shows how all animals and plants have come to be as they are today through the process of evolution. His idea is called natural selection, and it describes the gradual development of all living things, from primitive life forms billions of years ago, to the present time. In his great book, *Origin of Species*, he sets out the ideas of natural selection and evolution.

Charles Darwin was born at Shrewsbury, in England, in 1809. He became interested in geology and natural history while studying theology at Cambridge University. He became friendly with a botanist, Professor J Henslow, who obtained for him the position of naturalist on the ship HMS *Beagle*, which was sailing to South America and the South Sea Islands to carry out coastline surveys. On the five-year voyage, Darwin studied thousands of animals and plants, and this provided him

During the five-year voyage on HMS Beagle, *Darwin travelled to South America and the South Sea Islands.*

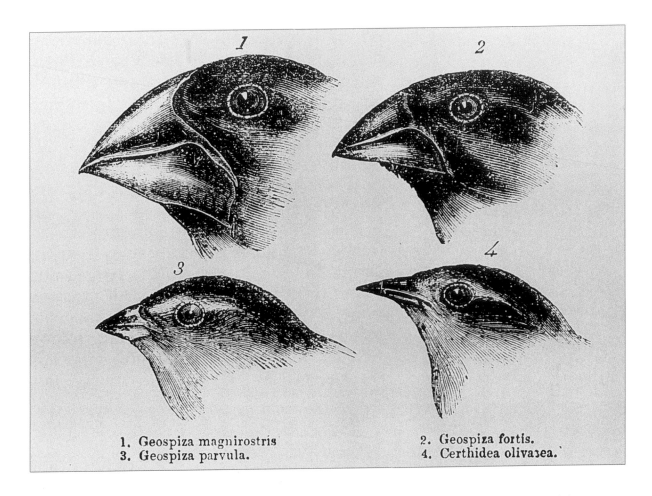

1. Geospiza magnirostris
3. Geospiza parvula.
2. Geospiza fortis.
4. Certhidea olivazea.

with scientific material to study for the rest of his life.

The ship's captain, Robert FitzRoy, was a firm believer in the biblical theory of creation. The Bible states that God created the world in seven days and that all the different animals and plants were created as they are now. FitzRoy hoped he had found 'a well-educated and scientific person' to travel on the *Beagle* who could make observations which would prove the correctness of this view of creation. However, as a result of his studies during the voyage, Darwin began to suspect that the biblical theory of creation was not correct.

Darwin returned to England in 1836, and set to work on his notes. By 1846, he had published an account describing his voyage

Darwin studied the beaks of the different types of finches found on the Galapagos Islands, off the west coast of South America. These gave him important clues about how different species developed.

on the *Beagle*, along with three important books about geology. He also began to think seriously about evolution and natural selection, and wrote two essays describing his ideas. He did not publish these essays because he realized his ideas proved the biblical theory of creation was wrong, and he was worried about the anger and uproar they would cause.

The term 'natural selection' means that there is a continual struggle among animals and plants to survive, and those that vary from others in a useful way will produce more offspring. Some of these offspring will inherit the useful characteristics and in turn will be able to produce more offspring themselves. As the process continues, the

During his visit to the Galapagos Islands, Darwin took the chance to study the many unusual animals and plants he found there, such as these giant tortoises.

As this cartoon, published in 1861, shows, many people thought that Darwin believed humans had evolved directly from apes.

typical features of the successful animals and plants will change gradually. Eventually a new species, a group that shares many characteristics and is only able to breed among themselves, will come into being.

In 1858, Darwin discovered that another naturalist, Alfred Russel Wallace, had also been thinking about the theory of evolution. A year later Darwin published a full account of his theory of evolution in his book *Origin of Species*. The book was widely read and created tremendous arguments and disagreements, but gradually many of Darwin's critics decided that his theory was right. Today, Darwin's theories provide the basis for our understanding of the process of evolution.

Dates

1809 born in Shrewsbury, England
1831 receives a BA degree in theology from Cambridge University and leaves on a voyage to South America and the South Sea Islands aboard the *Beagle*
1836 returns to England
1839 publishes a journal of the *Beagle* voyage
1842 writes his first essay on the origin of species
1859 publishes the *Origin of Species*
1882 dies

Louis *Pasteur*

Vaccination to fight disease

Before Louis Pasteur carried out his research in the mid-1800s, doctors did not have a clear idea about how diseases and infections were caused. They also had no way to prevent disease. Through his careful experiments with microbes, Pasteur showed how these tiny living things can be passed to people and animals through water, food and air. This convinced him that microbes are what cause diseases and infections, and that they could be controlled. He developed a technique called vaccination, which helps people and animals to build up a resistance to certain microbes and so gives protection against disease.

Louis Pasteur examining specimens in his laboratory. He experimented on animals when he was developing his vaccines.

When Pasteur worked on the deadly disease rabies, he carried out experiments on dogs who had the disease.

Louis Pasteur's first interest was in chemistry – the study of the way everything combines and reacts with each other. In 1847, when he was studying crystals, he made his first big discovery. He found that crystals that are chemically the same could have different shapes, because of how the molecules, the small particles which make them up, fit together. He also showed that the way the molecules fit together affects the chemical nature of a substance.

In 1854, Pasteur was appointed head of the science department at the University of Lille in northern France. There were many breweries in Lille, and he soon became interested in the process called fermentation, which produces alcohol, and why beers and wines go sour and become undrinkable. Pasteur showed that yeast cells were responsible for the fermentation, and that bacteria caused the beer or wine to spoil.

In the course of his work, Pasteur showed that the bacteria could be killed by moderate heat. This led to the development of the process of pasteurization, which is a method of preventing milk and other liquids from going bad, by heating the liquid and holding it at a high temperature for a certain amount of time.

Above   Pasteur discovered that it was possible to make a vaccine against rabies by using the dried body fluids from a rabbit that had the disease.

Right   The first person to receive the rabies vaccine was a young boy who had been bitten by a dog with the disease. The vaccine saved his life.

His work on fermentation convinced Pasteur that microbes must be involved in many other chemical processes, and that they might be responsible for diseases in humans and animals. In 1876, a German doctor, Robert Koch, proved that Pasteur's theory was right, when he showed that a specific microbe causes a specific disease.

Pasteur made an important discovery when he was working on the anthrax bacteria, a microbe which causes a deadly disease in cattle and humans. He injected chicks with weak anthrax bacteria. This allowed the chicks to develop defences, or resistence, against the bacteria. When the chicks were then exposed to the bacteria, they did not die. Instead they had developed a resistance to the disease. Pasteur quickly realized that by inoculating people and animals with weakened bacteria it would be possible to prevent many other types of diseases.

Pasteur became convinced that vaccines were the best hope of conquering disease, and he continued to work on them for the rest of his life. His work led to the development of a vaccination against the deadly disease of rabies in humans and animals, as well as a successful vaccine against a disease called diphtheria.

When Pasteur died in 1895, several serious diseases had been conquered thanks to his efforts. The science of vaccines pioneered by Pasteur is still one of the most powerful methods in the fight against disease.

Dates

1827 born in Dôle, France
1844 studies the chemical make up of crystals
1854 appointed head of the science department at Lille University, France
1864 invents the process of pasteurization
1879 discovers the principles of vaccination
1881 demonstrates a successful vaccine against rabies
1895 dies

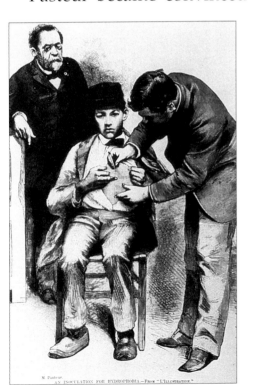

M. Pasteur.
AN INOCULATION FOR HYDROPHOBIA.—FROM "L'ILLUSTRATION."

Marie *Curie*

Revealing the power of the atom

Marie Sklodowska was born in 1867 in Warsaw, Poland. From childhood she longed to study science, but at that time girls were not allowed to attend Polish universities, and Marie's parents did not have enough money to send her to university abroad. But Marie was determined, and found a job as a governess to earn the money that she needed.

Marie Curie and her husband, Pierre, will always be remembered among the earliest workers in the science of radioactivity, which has to do with the powerful rays that some substances give off. Despite the great difficulties they worked under – they spent most of their money on apparatus and materials and often did not have enough food to eat – they made some remarkable discoveries. Marie continued to work after the death of Pierre, and became the first scientist to receive two Nobel Prizes.

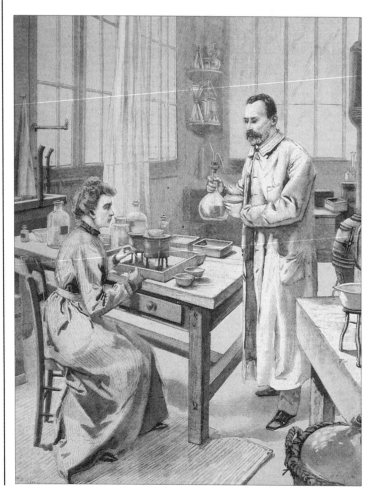

At the beginning of her scientific career, Marie Curie worked in a laboratory with her husband Pierre.

After three years of working, Marie had saved enough money to study science at the Sorbonne – the University of Paris, France. While there, she met Pierre Curie, a physicist, and in 1895 they were married. Marie then began working for a PhD degree, studying rays similar to X-rays which are given off by the element uranium. She called this giving off of rays radioactivity.

In the course of her work, Marie also discovered a new, even more radioactive, element. She named this element polonium, after her native country, Poland. Soon Pierre joined Marie in her work and together they obtained a pure sample of polonium. They also discovered radium, another radioactive

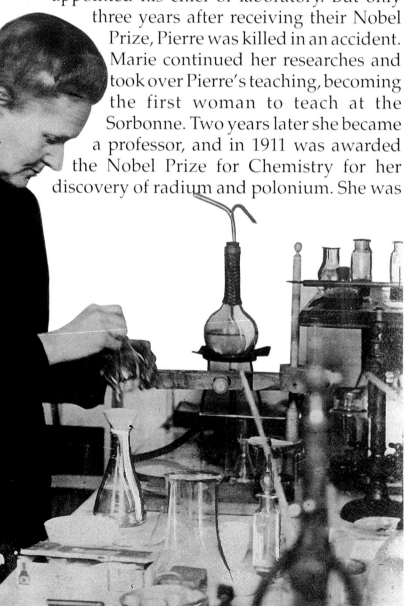

After Pierre's death, Marie continued her work on radioactivity.

element, which is a million times more radioactive than uranium. Marie earned her PhD degree with this work in 1903, and became the first woman to receive this degree in Europe. In the same year, she and Pierre shared the Nobel Prize for Physics for their work on radioactivity with the French physicist Henri Becquerel. Marie was the first woman to win a Nobel Prize.

Soon afterwards, Pierre was made a special professor at the Sorbonne and Marie was appointed his chief of laboratory. But only three years after receiving their Nobel Prize, Pierre was killed in an accident. Marie continued her researches and took over Pierre's teaching, becoming the first woman to teach at the Sorbonne. Two years later she became a professor, and in 1911 was awarded the Nobel Prize for Chemistry for her discovery of radium and polonium. She was the first scientist to receive two Nobel Prizes. She was also given charge of a laboratory at the newly built Institute of Radium in Paris.

Marie worked at the Institute for the rest of her life. Her example made many people realize the importance of science, and she used her fame to raise money for scientific research. But Marie was never fully aware of the health dangers associated with the radioactive elements she studied, and she died in 1934, at the age of sixty-seven, from a form of blood disease caused by radioactivity.

Dates

1867 born in Warsaw, Poland
1891 enrols at the Sorbonne in Paris, France
1894 receives a degree in mathematics
1895 marries Pierre Curie
1902 Marie and Pierre purify radium
1903 awarded Nobel Prize for Physics jointly with Pierre and Henri Becquerel
1911 awarded Nobel Prize for Chemistry
1934 dies

Marie Curie was the first woman to teach at the Sorbonne.

Albert *Einstein*

The father of modern physics

Albert Einstein was one of the greatest scientific thinkers of all time. His work laid the foundation of modern physics and still forms the basis of how we interpret the universe and the things that scientists see in it. His ideas have led to the discovery of very different things, ranging from nuclear power to black holes in space. Throughout his life Einstein was against war and worked for peace.

Albert Einstein was born of Jewish parents in 1879 in Ulm, in southern Germany, and he went to school in Munich. He did badly at school, but was fascinated by mathematics, at which he excelled. When he was fifteen, his family moved to Milan, Italy, and from there he went on to attend the Polytechnic of Zurich, in Switzerland.

After gaining a teaching qualification from the Polytechnic, Einstein took a post as a junior clerk in the Swiss patent office in Bern. Einstein was happy to work at such an easy

Albert Einstein (seated left) with a group of student friends.

Einstein with his first wife Mileva. Mileva was a mathematician and Einstein often discussed his ideas with her.

job, because it gave him plenty of time to think about physics. It was the 'thought experiments' that he carried out in his head that led to a new understanding of space, time and gravity.

In 1905, when he was twenty-six years old, Einstein began to publish his thoughts. One of his theories provided an explanation for a puzzling effect, called the photoelectric effect, that had been noticed some years earlier. It was known that when light was shone on certain substances, the substances gave out minute electrically-charged particles called electrons. Einstein's explanation suggested that light, as well as moving in waves, actually came in separate little 'packets' of energy, later called photons. He was awarded the Nobel Prize for Physics in 1921 for his work on the photo-electric effect.

Einstein also developed his theories of general and special relativity. These theories were so different and new that most scientists could not believe or understand them and it took a long time for them to be accepted.

The theory of special relativity describes what would happen to objects travelling very fast, at speeds near the speed of light. At such speeds Einstein's theory showed that distances shrink and time slows down. His theory of general relativity is about the effects of gravity and puts forward the idea of space-time, which is a combination of space and time. This work predicted that light would be bent by the force of gravity, and that time would slow down where the force of gravity is strong. Both of these ideas have since been shown to be true by experiments, and provide useful clues to the understanding of the universe.

Einstein's theories also predicted that solid objects can be changed into pure energy. This led to the development of nuclear power and the atomic bomb. However, Einstein himself protested against nuclear weapons, and became involved in the peace movement after the First World War (1914-18).

This picture illustrates the idea that space is distorted by gravity – an idea that is the consequence of Einstein's theory of general relativity.

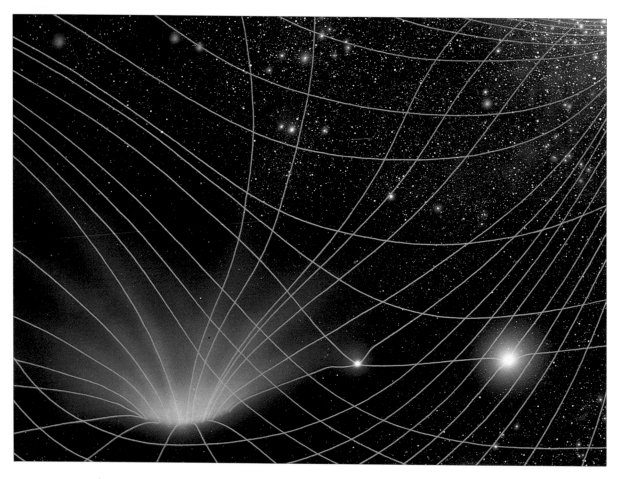

The 4 Equations

$$g_{ik;l} = 0; \quad \Gamma_i = 0$$

$$R_{ik} = 0; \quad g_{is}^{is} = 0$$

In 1914 Einstein had been appointed Research Director at the University of Berlin, in Germany. However, in 1933, he left Germany because of the Nazi Party's anti-Jewish activities and went to live in the United States. In 1941, he became a citizen of the United States.

Although Einstein was one of the greatest scientists who ever lived, he did not take himself too seriously. Once, when asked to enter a newspaper competition to write an article explaining how light is bent by gravity, he joked that the competition was much too difficult for him to enter. When he died in 1955 at the age of seventy-six, he left behind a wealth of ideas that form the basis of modern physics today.

Dates

1879 born in Ulm, Germany
1900 graduates from the Polytechnic of Zurich, Switzerland
1902 starts work in patent office in Bern, Switzerland
1905 publishes the *Special Theory of Relativity*
1914 becomes Research Director at University of Berlin
1916 publishes the *General Theory of Relativity*
1921 wins the Nobel Prize for Physics for his work on the photoelectric effect
1933 moves permanently to Princeton University in the United States
1941 becomes a US citizen
1955 dies

Margaret *Mead*

Understanding the lives of other peoples

Margaret Mead was one of the first women to go to a remote part of the world to study the lives of the people who lived there. Through her work, she was able to show people of western 'developed' countries that much could be learned from the daily lives and the values of so-called 'primitive' peoples. Mead said, 'I have spent most of my life studying the lives of other peoples . . . so that (westerners) might better understand themselves.'

In order to study the origins, religious beliefs, social relationships and other ways of humans, scientists called anthropologists need to live and work with the people they study. This presented a great problem for Margaret Mead. After she received her PhD in anthropology in 1925, she was eager to continue her study of the people of the

Margaret Mead's work helped ordinary people to understand the importance of learning about other cultures.

Polynesian islands in the South Pacific. But in those days it was considered too dangerous for a young woman to go alone to a remote part of the world.

In spite of the difficulties, Mead went off to work in Samoa, a group of South Pacific islands. She chose Samoa because not many westerners had visited the islands, and so the traditional activities and ideas of many of the Samoan people would be unchanged by 'modern' ways of doing things. When she arrived, she went to the largely unspoiled island of Ta'u and she soon learned that the best way to gain information about how the Samoans lived was to learn their language, and to take part in the daily life of the people.

In Samoa, Mead noticed that children were cared for not only by their mothers but also by aunts, uncles, grandparents and older children.

Through her investigations, she found that in Samoa children were brought up with different values to the ones she knew. In Ta'u children were cared for not only by their parents, but also by older children as well as aunts, uncles and grandparents. She also noticed that Samoan teenagers were generally happy and carefree. In the United States and other western countries, teenagers tended to be anxious and rebellious, and this was generally thought to be an unavoidable part of becoming an adult.

Mead published her findings in 1928, in *Coming of Age in Samoa*. The book became an instant bestseller in the United States, but it also upset many people because it challenged what they had been taught about sex, love, marriage and

Mead's work in Papua New Guinea helped people around the world to understand their own lives better.

family values. The book also introduced the science of anthropology to ordinary people, who could now see how studying the lives of other people could help them to understand their own lives. It also made people think about how patterns of behaviour develop in societies – is behaviour inherited from parents or relatives, or are people more influenced by what goes on around them?

Throughout her career, Mead continued to carry out her work in the South Pacific, Indonesia and the West Indies, and to write about her findings. The techniques she used paved the way for other anthropologists, and helped to bring an understanding of anthropology and other cultures to people around the world.

Dates

1901 born in Philadelphia, Pennsylvania, USA
1925 receives her PhD in anthropology from Columbia University in New York, and sets off for Samoa
1928 *Coming of Age in Samoa* is published; begins field work in New Guinea
1929 writes *Growing up in New Guinea*
1936 field work in Bali
1942 publishes *Balinese Character*, written with Gregory Bateson
1972 publishes her autobiography, *Blackberry Winter*
1978 dies

Linus *Pauling*

Outstanding chemist of the twentieth century

The chemist, Linus Pauling, made outstanding contributions to the understanding of the structure of molecules. His work led him to believe that huge doses of vitamin C – a substance found in lemons, oranges and other citrus fruits, and vegetables – would cure the common cold and even some forms of cancer. When he won his second Nobel Prize in 1962, he was the only person to have won two Nobel Prizes without sharing one or both with another person.

Linus Pauling was born in Portland, Oregon, in the United States, and from an early age began experimenting with chemicals. He studied chemistry at what is now Oregon State University, and graduated in 1922. While working for his PhD, Pauling studied the structure or framework of minerals and other inorganic molecules, using X-ray crystallography. In this technique, X-rays are shone

Linus Pauling's work greatly advanced our understanding of the structure of molecules.

through a crystal and the patterns produced are then examined to determine the crystal structure. He also developed a way of finding out the structure of many different minerals.

After he received his PhD, Pauling spent two years in Germany where he made some important breakthroughs in the understanding of chemical bonds, the links which hold atoms together in molecules. He published the main points of this work in 1939 in his book, *The Nature of the Chemical Bond*, which is one of the most influential science books of the twentieth century.

When Pauling returned to the United States, he turned his attention to understanding

Pauling used techniques, such as X-ray crystallography, to determine the structure of complicated molecules. Examining crystals of substances using a special kind of microscope can also reveal important information. These are crystals of vitamin C.

Dates

1901 born in Portland, Oregon, USA
1925 awarded a PhD in chemistry from the California Institute of Technology
1926 studies in Germany
1927 returns to the USA
1939 publishes *The Nature of the Chemical Bond*
1954 wins the Nobel Prize for Chemistry
1958 presents a petition against nuclear weapons to the United Nations
1962 wins the Nobel Peace Prize

how the molecules in our bodies work. He began by using X-ray crystallography to find out the exact shape of amino acids and peptides, two building blocks of protein molecules. Proteins are an essential part of the body and are found in all tissues. They are important for growth and repair of the body. He used the information to help him to come up with a model for the structure of proteins.

In 1949, Pauling suggested that the inherited disease, sickle cell anaemia, is caused by a change in the content of red blood cells. This was the first time anyone had ever traced the origin of a disease down to molecules. Pauling's work also convinced him of the value of large doses of vitamin C in maintaining good health.

But Pauling was more than just a chemist. He also campaigned for world peace and protested against the testing of nuclear weapons. In 1958, he presented a petition protesting against nuclear testing to the United Nations signed by more than 11,000 scientists. In 1954, he was awarded the Nobel Prize for Chemistry for his work on chemical bonding, and in 1962 he won the Nobel Peace Prize.

Dorothy *Hodgkin*

Revealing the structure of crystals

Dorothy Hodgkin worked to find out about the structure of different substances in our bodies. Once the structure of substances has been found, then scientists are able to discover the job they perform, for example, in the body, where they can help in fighting off diseases and infections. Her work has also led to the understanding of how drugs work and how to design new drugs in the fight against disease.

Dorothy Hodgkin's interest in chemistry started at the age of fifteen, when she was given a chemistry set. In 1928, she went to Oxford University to study chemistry. In those days, few women chose to study a science subject, let alone chemistry, which required an extra year of study.

During her fourth year at Oxford, Hodgkin became very interested in X-ray crystallography. In this technique, X-rays are shone through crystals and the pattern of dark spots

Dorothy Hodgkin used X-ray crystallography to determine the structure of many complicated molecules.

Hodgkin receiving the Nobel Prize in 1964, for her work on the structure of vitamin B12.

that results, reveals the internal structure of the crystals. When Dorothy Hodgkin began her work, most of the process had to be carried out by hand. Today, X-ray crystallography is done mainly by machines, and computers are used to work out the structure of the crystals – a technique she pioneered.

From 1942 to 1945, Hodgkin worked on discovering the structure of penicillin, a 'wonder drug' which was first discovered in 1928. Penicillin is an antibiotic, which means that it is used to help cure diseases caused by bacteria – tiny organisms that can be seen under a microscope.

In 1956, after eight years of hard work, she succeeded in discovering the structure of vitamin B12, a complicated molecule which contains more than ninety atoms. Atoms are the smallest parts of a molecule, and the more atoms there are in a molecule, the more difficult it is to find out its structure. By 1969, with the aid of computer technology, she was able to work out the structure of insulin. Insulin is a chemical substance which controls the amount of sugar in the blood, and is made up of more than 800 atoms.

Hodgkin married in 1937, and became a mother while at the same time teaching and following a successful research career. In 1964, she won the Nobel Prize for Chemistry, and the following year she became the first woman since Florence Nightingale to be awarded the Order of Merit.

After she retired from active research, Hodgkin travelled widely to discuss science and work for international peace and understanding. She now lives in a village near Oxford, England.

Dates

1910 born in Cairo, Egypt, to British parents
1928 admitted to Somerville College at Oxford University to read chemistry
1931 begins working on X-ray crystallography
1945 determines the structure of penicillin
1956 determines the structure of vitamin B_{12}
1964 wins the Nobel Prize for Chemistry
1965 awarded the Order of Merit
1969 determines the structure of insulin

Dorothy Hodgkin and fellow Nobel prize winner Alexander Prochozov (right) meet to discuss an appeal for peace in 1985.

James D *Watson*

Unravelling the structure of DNA

DNA is the material in most living things that passes on information, so that a creature's offspring looks very much like its parents. Until the chemical structure of DNA was known, it was not possible to understand how this large and complicated molecule was able to pass the information on. The work of James D Watson and his colleague Francis Crick provided the key to understanding how inherited characteristics, including inherited diseases, are passed on from parent to child.

James D Watson was born in 1928 in Chicago, Illinois, in the United States, and studied zoology at Indiana University. In 1951, after he completed his PhD, he went to work at the Cavendish Laboratories at Cambridge University in England.

This was an exciting time to be at the Cavendish Laboratories because the scientists there were using X-ray crystallography to study the structure of complicated molecules. One of the molecules the Cambridge scientists had been able to 'photograph' was DNA (deoxyribonucleic acid). DNA contains, in 'code', the information which controls what a living thing, or organism, will be like. For many years, scientists puzzled over the structure of DNA, for until this was known,

James D Watson, together with Francis Crick, discovered the structure of DNA, the molecule that determines our inherited characteristics.

Watson and Crick used X-ray diffraction patterns to gain basic information about the structure of DNA, and then used small balls and sticks to build up a three-dimensional model of the molecule.

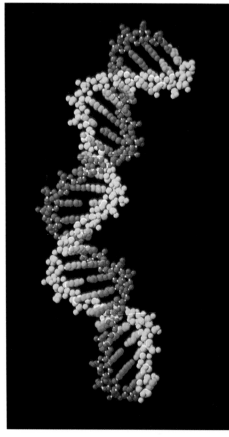

The DNA molecule has a double helix structure. It is shaped like a spiral staircase with steps made up of pairs of molecules that bind together in a special way.

it was not possible to understand how this molecule was able to pass on instructions for building a new organism.

Watson soon teamed up with the British scientist Francis Crick to try to work out the structure of DNA. They started by making a careful study of the X-ray patterns, and then, using small balls and sticks, tried to construct a three-dimensional model of DNA which included all its known features.

Other scientists, including the chemist Linus Pauling in the United States, also became interested in the structure of DNA – the race to discover the structure of DNA was on! After an exciting and nerve-wracking time wondering whether they would be the first people to work out the structure, Watson and Crick had a burst of inspiration. They realized that the DNA molecule must be arranged in a double spiral (helix), like two long springs wound round each other.

Within weeks, Watson and Crick had published their results in the British science journal *Nature*. It became clear that they had found a structure that not only made sense chemically, but also suggested how DNA copied itself, and so provided the key to how inherited characteristics are passed on. This knowledge is now helping scientists to fight inherited diseases and develop techniques, such as genetic fingerprinting, that can identify a person from a sample of his or her blood or tissue. Watson and Crick were awarded the Nobel Prize for Physiology or Medicine in 1962 for their part in the discovery. They shared the prize with the biochemist Maurice Wilkins, who worked on purifying and 'photographing' DNA.

Watson later returned to the United States where he continued to work on the genetic code contained in DNA. In 1968 he was made director of the famous Cold Spring Harbor Laboratory in New York. He went on to work at the National Institutes for Health in Washington, DC, where, until mid-1992, he led an American project aimed at understanding the location of all the genes in the human body.

Dates

1928 born in Chicago, Illinois, USA
1947 graduates from the University of Chicago with a degree in zoology
1950 obtains his PhD
1951 goes to work at the Cavendish Laboratory at Cambridge University, England
1953 constructs a molecular model of DNA (with Francis Crick)
1962 awarded the Nobel Prize for Physiology or Medicine jointly with Francis Crick and Maurice Wilkins for their work on DNA
1968 becomes director of Cold Spring Harbor Laboratory in New York
1988 appointed head of the Office for Human Genome Research in Washington, DC

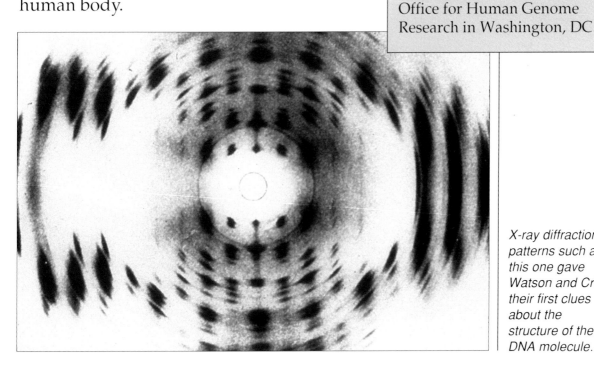

X-ray diffraction patterns such as this one gave Watson and Crick their first clues about the structure of the DNA molecule.

Richard *Feynman*

Finding the fun in physics

Richard Feynman was one of the world's greatest theoretical physicists – people who come up with ideas to explain such things as magnetism, light and electricity. He won the Nobel Prize for his contribution to a theory called quantum electrodynamics, which can be used to prove all known rules or laws in physics about electricity, mechanics and chemistry, and to predict the existence of new types of atomic particles.

Richard Feynman was born in 1918 in a small town near New York City in the United States. He loved experimenting as a child, and went on to study physics at university. While he was a PhD student at Princeton University, he was asked to join the Manhattan Project.

Richard Feynman was known for his enthusiastic style of lecturing, which inspired his listeners to find out more about the world around them.

The first explosion of an atomic bomb at a test site in New Mexico in 1945. Feynman worked with a team of physicists on the Manhatten Project, which led to this atomic bomb test.

The Manhattan Project was a secret American project to develop the atomic bomb. It was started after German scientists discovered that the centre or nucleus of an atom could be split into parts, and many people began to worry that the leader of Germany, Adolf Hitler, would build an atomic bomb. The Manhattan Project was based in a top-security laboratory near Los Alamos, New Mexico, in the southwestern United States. The result of this was the first explosion of an atomic bomb, which took place at a test site in New Mexico on 16 July 1945.

After the Manhattan Project ended, Feynman went to teach first at Cornell University in New York, and later at the California Institute of Technology. During this time he worked to understand how fundamental forces, such as light, electricity and magnetism, work together. To try to solve the problem, he applied mathematics to the study of the nature of atomic particles. This contributed greatly to the development of the theory of quantum electrodynamics, or QED, an important theory in physics.

In 1986, Feynman was asked to serve on the committee investigating the cause of the *Challenger* space shuttle disaster. Early on in the investigation, he became convinced that cold weather had caused the O-ring seals

One of the booster rockets veers out of control following the explosion that destroyed the Space Shuttle *Challenger in* 1986.

between the sections of the space shuttle's solid fuel boosters to fail. This allowed hot gas to leak and burn a hole through the tank containing explosive liquid hydrogen, thus causing the explosion.

To prove his point, Feynman conducted a simple, but dramatic, experiment. During one committee session he cooled a sample of the O-ring rubber seal in a glass of iced water, and demonstrated how it failed to spring back when removed from the water. He argued that the same sort of failure had caused the O-rings on the *Challenger* to leak.

Feynman loved any kind of puzzle and gained a reputation as a brilliant story teller, a practical joker and a lively bongo drum player. He was awarded the Nobel Prize for Physics in 1965, for his work on quantum electrodynamics, and inspired many students with his enthusiastic style of lecturing and his love of life. He died of cancer in 1988.

Dates

1918 born in Far Rockaway, New York, USA
1935 goes to the Massachusetts Institute of Technology to study physics
1939 goes to Princeton University to study for a PhD
1943 goes to Los Alamos to work on the Manhattan Project
1945 first explosion of an atomic bomb
1965 wins the Nobel Prize for Physics for his work on quantum electrodynamics
1986 serves on the committee investigating the *Challenger* space shuttle disaster
1988 dies

Stephen *Hawking*

Searching to understand the universe

Confined to a wheelchair for the last twenty-five years, Stephen Hawking is one of the world's leading thinkers on the origin and nature of the universe. He is best known for his work on black holes – regions in space of very strong gravity caused by the collapse of stars. His contribution to physics has made him widely regarded as one of the most brilliant scientific thinkers since Einstein.

As a child growing up in St Albans, England, Stephen Hawking was inspired by his father, a specialist in tropical diseases, to become a scientist. But instead of taking up medicine, Hawking chose physics.

After receiving a degree in physics at Oxford University in 1962, Hawking went on to Cambridge to study for a PhD. While he was still a student, he discovered that he was suffering from motor neurone disease, an illness that leads to weakness and wasting of the muscles. The doctors gave him only years to live, and Hawking says that this threat of

Although he is confined to a wheelchair and can only speak with the aid of a computer, Stephen Hawking continues to be a popular lecturer.

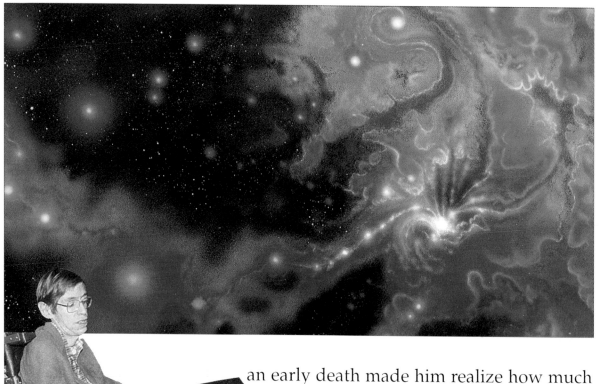

One of Hawking's great interests is black holes, regions in space where the force of gravity is so great that anything which falls into them will never come out again.

an early death made him realize how much there was to find out about how the universe works, and inspired him to make the most of his life.

Although he is now confined to a wheelchair and must speak with the aid of computers and a device that produces an electronic 'voice', Hawking has gone on to marry, have children and further our understanding of the mysteries of the universe.

After receiving his PhD in 1965, Hawking remained at Cambridge. In 1979 he was appointed the Lucasian Professor of Mathematics, a post once held by Isaac Newton. For much of his career he has concentrated on studying cosmology, a science which attempts to understand the creation, evolution and current structure of the universe.

One of his first interests was in black holes, regions in space where the force of gravity is so great that anything which falls into them will never come out again. Using mathematical calculations, which he does in his head, Hawking has shown that physics inside black holes has some features in common with physical forces here on earth.

He also predicted that black holes, from which nothing normally escapes, can give off heat. He is now working to understand the role of gravity in the workings of the universe, and on the theory of 'wormholes', tiny fluctuations in space which link together many different universes.

In 1988 Stephen Hawking published his book, *A Brief History of Time*. In this book, he tried to summarize his theories about black holes and the universe so that ordinary people can grasp their meaning. Although Hawking admits that most people will not understand everything in his book, he believes that many people are interested in the workings of the universe, and that everyone will learn something. His book has sold millions of copies all over the world, and proved him right.

Dates

1942 born in Oxford, England
1965 awarded a PhD from Cambridge University
1974 becomes a Fellow of the Royal Society, and shows that black holes can give out heat
1979 becomes Lucasian Professor of Mathematics at Cambridge
1988 publishes *A Brief History of Time*, which turns out to be a surprise best-seller

Hawking receives a certificate from the Guiness Book of Records *for his best-selling book,* A Brief History of Time.

Glossary

Anthropology   The study of the origins and cultural behaviour of human beings.

Apprenticed   Sent to work with a craftsman to learn a skill.

Atoms   The smallest particles of an element.

Bacteria   Microscopic organisms which are present everywhere, including in the human body.

Bookbinder   Someone who binds pages together to make a book.

Botanist   A scientist who studies plants.

Community   A group of plants and animals that live together and affect each other's lives.

Crystal   A solid substance with a particular shape, due to the arrangement of atoms or molecules of which it is made.

Diffraction   The splitting up of light.

Drugs   Chemical compounds that have an effect on living things.

Electric current   The flow of electricity.

Electrons   Particles in an atom which have a negative electric charge.

Element   A basic substance which can form part of a chemical compound.

Evolution   The gradual change in the characteristics of animals and plants over a long period.

Genes   Units of the body responsible for passing on characteristics from parents to offspring.

Geology   The study of the surface and interior of the earth.

Gravitation   The force of attraction of all objects to each other.

Inorganic   Describing compounds, such as minerals, that do not have the structure or characteristics of living things.

Laws   Rules that predict how things work, or what events will take place.

Lenses   Specially shaped pieces of glass, or other material, through which light can travel and which bend light rays.

Magnetic field   The area affected by the force of a magnet.

Microbe   Tiny forms of life, such as bacteria. Many microbes cause disease.

Natural history   The study of the world around us.

Nazi Party   A political party, led by Adolf Hitler, in the 1930s and 1940s. The Nazis believed that the German race was superior to most other people, and they behaved with great cruelty especially to Jewish people.

Nobel Prizes   Prizes awarded each year for outstanding achievements.

Nuclear energy   The energy released by the splitting of certain atoms.

Particles   Tiny pieces of matter.

PhD   An advanced university degree.

Physicist   A scientist who specializes in the branch of science called physics.

Plague   A deadly disease that killed many thousands of people in the past.

Predict   To suggest what will happen.

Principles   Basic rules.

Prism   A three-sided piece of glass or other material through which light can travel.

Relativity   A theory developed by Albert Einstein which describes the relationship between space, time and gravity.

Theology   The study of religions.

Theory   An explanation which may be correct but which has not been proved.

Three-dimensional   Having three dimensions – height, width and depth.

Uranium   A radioactive element which is sometimes used as a source of nuclear energy.

Vaccines   Material derived from disease-causing microbes or the chemicals they produce, which is injected into people and animals in order to make them resistant to the disease.

Voltage Electrical force.

X-rays A type of radiation which is able to pass through objects that light cannot penetrate.

Yeast A type of organism which can convert sugar into alcohol. It is also used in baking to make bread rise.

Books to read

Marie Curie by Andrew Dunn (Wayland, 1990)
Marie Curie, the Polish Scientist who Discovered Radium by Beverly Birch
   (Exley, 1988)
Charles Darwin and Evolution by Bernard Stonehouse (Wayland, 1981)
Disease and Discovery by Eva Bailey (Batsford, 1985)
Einstein for Beginners by J Schwartz and M McGuinness
   (Allen and Unwin, 1986)
Albert Einstein by Peter Lafferty (Wayland, 1991)
Michael Faraday by Michael Brophy (Wayland, 1990)
Focus on Electricity by Mark Lambert (Wayland, 1988)
Margaret Mead by Michael Pollard (Exley Publications, 1992)
Louis Pasteur by Nina Morgan (Wayland, 1991)
Isaac Newton by Douglas McTavish (Wayland, 1990)

For older readers
A Brief History of Time by Stephen Hawking (Bantum, 1988)
The Double Helix by James D. Watson (revised edn edited by Gunther Stent,
   Weidenfeld and Nicholson, London, 1981) (an exciting story for
   older readers)
Stephen Hawking: A Life in Science by Michael White and John Gribben
   (Viking, 1992) (an adult biography with excellent explanations of the
   scientific concepts)
Surely you're joking, Mr Feynman by Richard Feynman (Unwin Paperbacks,
   1986)
What do you care what other people think? by Richard Feynman (Unwin
   Paperbacks, 1990)
What Mad Pursuit by Francis Crick (Weidenfeld and Nicholson Ltd,
   London, 1989) (Crick's version of the discovery of the structure of DNA)

Index